Earth's Water

Text by Michèle Mira Pons
Illustrated by Sophie Lebot
and Laurent Audouin

Published in 2010 by Windmill Books, LLC
303 Park Avenue South, Suite # 1280, New York, NY 10010-3657

Adaptations to North American Edition © 2010 Windmill Books
Copyright © Éditions MILAN 2005

CREDITS:
Written by Michèle Mira Pons
Illustrated by Sophie Lebot and Laurent Audouin

Library of Congress Cataloging-in-Publication Data

Pons, Michèle Mira.
  Earth's water / text by Michèle Mira Pons ; illustrations by Sophie Lebot and Laurent Audouin. – North American ed.
      p. cm. – (Taking action for my planet)
   ISBN 978-1-60754-798-3 (library binding)
   1. Water–Environmental aspects. 2. Hydrologic cycle I. Lebot, Sophie. II. Audouin, Laurent. III. Title.
   GB662.3.P687 2010
   333.91–dc22

                              2009041398

Manufactured in the United States of America

CPSIA Compliance Information: Batch #BW10W: For further information
contact Windmill Books, New York, New York at 1-866-478-0556.

an imprint of
WINDMILL BOOKS.
New York

Charter for the Environment

The Congress recognizes that each person should enjoy a healthful environment and that each person has a responsibility to contribute to the preservation and enhancement of the environment.

–The National Environmental Policy Act of 1969, Section 101(c)

TABLE OF CONTENTS

Words marked with an asterisk (*) when first used are explained in the glossary on p.30.

Water, Our "Blue Gold," Must Be Protected

Water is essential for all life on Earth. Without water, life would never have appeared on our planet, which it did around 3 billion years ago. All living beings are made up of water. In fact, 65% of our bodies are made of this precious liquid. Water is not only necessary to our survival, since we must drink it to live, but also for our daily comfort.

The Earth looks blue from outer space. That's because 71% of the Earth's surface is covered with water! The amount of freshwater available on our "blue planet" must provide for all Earth's inhabitants. However, many people lack water, especially in Africa and the Middle East. As only 10% of the countries on Earth hold 60% of the world's freshwater resources, this "blue gold" can become a cause for war. It has already caused conflicts in some regions.

In order for water to be shared fairly, water resources should be used in a sustainable, well-planned way. But that is not always the case. Water resources are often poorly managed. Overuse, waste, pollution, selfishness and lack of respect for others are typical ways in which water is misused. However, everyone can help contribute to the protection and maintenance of our water resources by taking small actions. This book will teach you more about water and how to protect this important resource.

? What is Water?

Our "blue planet" was formed about 4.5 billion years ago. Later (about 3 billion years ago), life on Earth first appeared — in the water — in the form of microscopic organisms. Later, other living creatures moved onto the land, but they always lived near a water source, for there is no life without water.

Everything Is Made of Water

Big or small, living in water or not, all living beings contain more water than they do any other substance. Our bodies, for example, are composed of around 65% water. Water is vital to our bodies and the sensation of thirst reminds us that we need to drink about 6-8 cups (1.5-2 L) a day to survive.

Water Is a Solvent

YOU WILL NEED:
- 2 glasses of water
- 1 lump of sugar
- 1 spoonful of salt

2. What do you observe? The sugar and salt have "dissolved" in the water, which will taste sugary or salty, even though both glasses look the same as before.

1. Stir the sugar in the first glass of water and stir the salt into the second. Mix well with a spoon.

Water also absorbs many pollutants that can't be seen with the naked eye.

White Gold
on the Blue Planet
Salt from the ocean has been mined from salt marshes since the Middle Ages.

The Properties of Water

Water has unique properties, some of which are well known. For example, water takes the form of whatever container holds it, such as a vase, a glass, a riverbed. Water dissolves numerous substances that then become invisible in the water. Sea water contains salt; freshwater contains other dissolved minerals, like calcium and magnesium.

WATER MAKES UP A CERTAIN PERCENTAGE OF EVERY LIVING THING.

A fish: 70%

A person: 65%

An octopus: 95%

A tomato: 91%

Potato: 78%

Frog: 78%

A head of lettuce: 95%

The majority of the Earth's water is salty - that is, ocean water. Humans cannot drink this type of water. Most freshwater comes from glaciers found at the Earth's poles and high in the mountains. Glaciers are formed by large quantities of snow that, pressed under their own weight, have turned into ice. Water has three states: solid, liquid, and gas.

liquid state

Liquid, Solid, Gas

70% of the water on Earth is in a liquid state: oceans, rivers, and also in rain, clouds or fog. Water is solid when it is transformed into ice at a temperature of 32° F (0° C) and in the forms of snow, frost, sleet and hail. Water can also be in a gaseous state, like water vapor. This is visible on glass when it's cold outside.

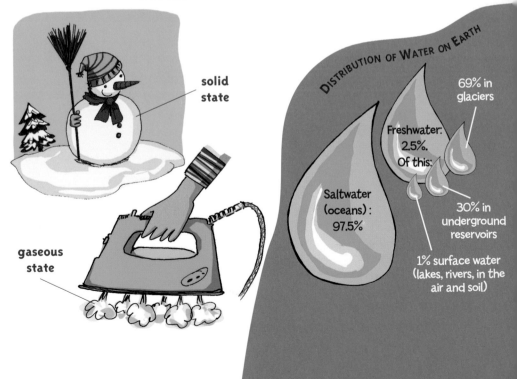

solid state

gaseous state

DISTRIBUTION OF WATER ON EARTH

69% in glaciers

Freshwater: 2.5%. Of this:

Saltwater (oceans): 97.5%

30% in underground reservoirs

1% surface water (lakes, rivers, in the air and soil)

Water You Don't See

Water seeps into the soil easily and is present everywhere in it. There is a great deal of water under our feet in the form of groundwater*. Sometimes this water rises to the surface, creating a spring. Water usually remains underground for around 20 years before it surfaces. Sometimes it stays underground for several centuries. When that happens, it is called "fossil water."

Spring

Aquifer

Calculate the Volume of Your Hand

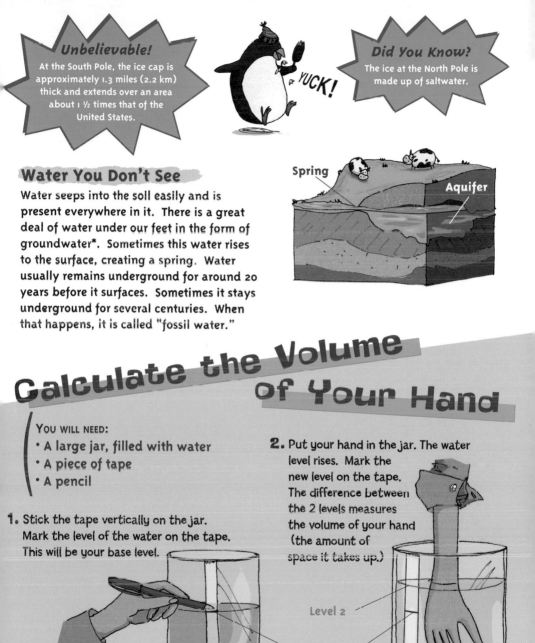

YOU WILL NEED:
- A large jar, filled with water
- A piece of tape
- A pencil

1. Stick the tape vertically on the jar. Mark the level of the water on the tape. This will be your base level.

2. Put your hand in the jar. The water level rises. Mark the new level on the tape. The difference between the 2 levels measures the volume of your hand (the amount of space it takes up.)

Level 2

Level 1

We owe this method of calculation to the great sage Archimedes. While taking a bath, he noticed that a body immersed in water displaces an amount of water equal to its own volume.

Water circulates between the ground and the sky.

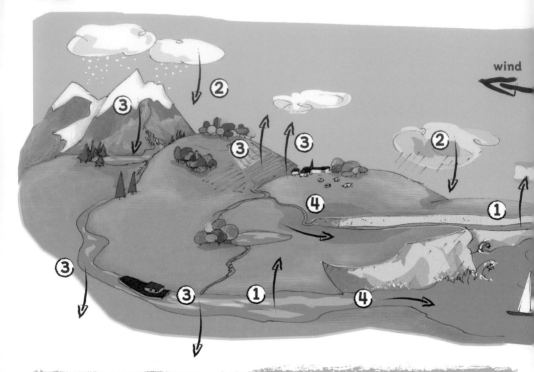

wind

WATER AND CLIMATE

When rivers run over their banks unexpectedly they often create disastrous floods. But areas that flood each year play an important role in nature because they act like reservoirs when the land later becomes hot and dry. In addition, the rainwater shapes the landscape. The water flows along, wearing away the soil, carving out narrow valleys and hollows in rocks.

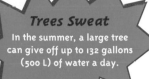

Trees Sweat

In the summer, a large tree can give off up to 132 gallons (500 L) of water a day.

Nile Flooding

Egyptian civilization was able to flourish thanks to the yearly flooding of the Nile River, which made the narrow strips of land on either side of the river extremely fertile.

① Warmed by the heat of the Sun's rays, the water of oceans, rivers, lakes — even the water contained in the soil and in plants — evaporates into water vapor.

② Clouds form in the sky, full of water droplets. When the temperature drops, the water droplets come together, become heavier and fall from the sky. That's rain (or snow, if it's very cold).

③ Some of the rain that falls on the ground evaporates again into the atmosphere, but some of it flows into rivers or seeps into the soil and ends up as groundwater.

④ Streams and layers of water also flow into the oceans and the cycle begins again.

Create Some Clouds

2. Cover the top of the glass jar with the plate. Place the ice cubes on the plate.

YOU WILL NEED:
• A kettle
• 1 heat-safe glass jar
• Water
• 1 plate
• Ice cubes

1. Have an adult bring water to a boil in the kettle. Pour it carefully into the heat-safe glass jar.

The water vapor in the glass jar collects in droplets on the bottom of the plate. This is how clouds form, as a result of water vapor condensing.

We drink water because it's necessary for our survival. Water provides our bodies with certain essential nutrients, like minerals. It also replenishes the water we lose when we sweat or urinate. These bodily functions are very important because they rid our bodies of waste products.

WATER AS MEDICINE

Since ancient times, certain springs have been famous for their medicinal properties.* The water in such springs accumulates minerals while underground. When the water springs to the surface, the water may be hot, or it may contain minerals that people believe help treat arthritis, respiratory problems, or kidney and skin diseases.

Around the House

We use water each day as we wash our hands before each meal, when we brush our teeth after meals, and when we flush the toilet. All of these daily habits that protect our health require water. We also wash our clothes, wash the dishes, and keep our floors clean with water.

How Much Water is Needed to Make...

It takes 105 gallons (400 L) of water to produce 5 lbs (2.2 kg) of paper.

It takes between 1,320 and 2,640 gallons (5,000-10,000 L) of water to make 1 car.

It takes 1.5 gallons (6 L) of water to make 5 lbs (2.2 kg) of candy.

From Field to Factory

Agriculture uses a lot of water. Fruits and vegetables need to be watered regularly in order to grow properly.

Industry uses a lot of water, too. Whether the factory is making products like paper, food products, chemicals, or refining oil — water is needed to wash, dissolve, extract and transform the raw materials into these products.

The Taste of Water

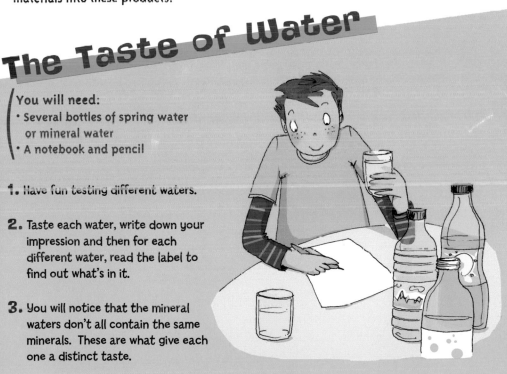

You will need:
- Several bottles of spring water or mineral water
- A notebook and pencil

1. Have fun testing different waters.

2. Taste each water, write down your impression and then for each different water, read the label to find out what's in it.

3. You will notice that the mineral waters don't all contain the same minerals. These are what give each one a distinct taste.

Tap water also contains minerals. It has been treated to make it safe to drink.

Water As an Energy Source

If you stick your hand in a river, you notice that it's pulled along by the current. Since ancient times, people have used the force of water current as a a power source. For example, water wheels have been used to sculpt stones, to grind materials and to make all sorts of products.

THE CASE AGAINST DAMS

People criticize dams for disturbing ecosystems. Big dams flood large areas of land, keep animal species from returning to their spawning grounds, create conditions that may increase disease and displace entire populations. One solution may be to construct much smaller dams.

Water as a Means of Transportation

Waterways have always played an important role in business and in the growth of cities. Rivers have long been used to transport goods. This is why so many large cities have grown next to rivers.

Make a Waterwheel

YOU WILL NEED:
- 2 round plastic lids from oatmeal containers
- 2 wooden dowels
- 2 rubber bands
- 2 Y-shaped pieces of wood

1. Cut a slit (half the diameter) in each box bottom. Fit the two pieces together. These are the sails of the waterwheel.

Canals

Where waterways do not exist naturally, people dig canals. In Central America, the Panama Canal connects the Atlantic Ocean to the Pacific Ocean.

Hydroelectricity

Hydroelectric power can be produced by the natural movement of water. This is a renewable energy source. Dams, which hold back a large amount of water, make use of the force of falling water. Other hydroelectric plants are powered by ocean tides, but these are less common because they are very difficult to install. Ways of generating power with ocean waves are still being studied.

The Biggest Dam

In order to construct the Three Gorges Dam in China, builders had to completely submerge more than 10 cities and relocate more than 2 million people.

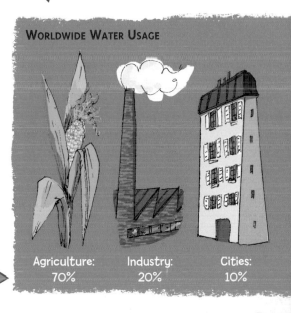

WORLDWIDE WATER USAGE

Agriculture: 70%   Industry: 20%   Cities: 10%

2. Join the 2 dowels and hold them together with the rubber bands. Slide the sails of the water wheel between the 2 dowels.

3. Set the 2 Y-shaped pieces of wood on either side of a little stream of water. Set what you have made into the forked pieces. The current of the water will make the sails of the water wheel turn one after the other.

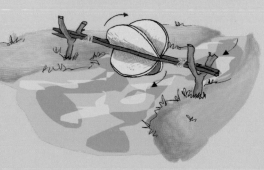

Tap Water

Today it seems normal to turn on the tap and see water flow out of it. But it's not really so simple. After having been pumped from underground aquifers, rivers or dams, water is treated and then piped toward our homes in underground water mains. In ancient times, the Romans devised a system of water distribution called aqueducts. Later, in the Middle Ages, water was distributed by water carriers who walked through the streets, selling water from the buckets they carried.

Make a Water Clock

YOU WILL NEED:
- 2 tall glasses
- A cardboard box a little taller than half the height of the glasses
- A long piece of cotton cord about as thick as your finger

1. Place the first glass on a table and the second one on the box, so that it is above the first one. Place one end of the piece of cotton cord inside the bottom of each glass. Fill the glass that sits higher with water.

2. Little by little, the cotton cord will get wet and the water will slowly move from the higher glass to the lower glass. In order to measure the time, all you have to do is note the water level every hour and make a mark on the glass.

The Romans and the Egyptians devised machines to measure time noting the flow of water from one vase to another. These machines are called *clepsydras*.

Water Is Treated...

Water taken from natural sources is not always safe to drink. It must be purified at a water treatment plant. There the water is filtered through a thick layer of sand, then disinfected using chemical products (chlorine or ozone) to kill germs.

....Then Stored and Distributed

Next the water is passed through miles of underground pipes, which connect to large reservoirs. From there, it goes through other water pipes, which distribute it to where people live.

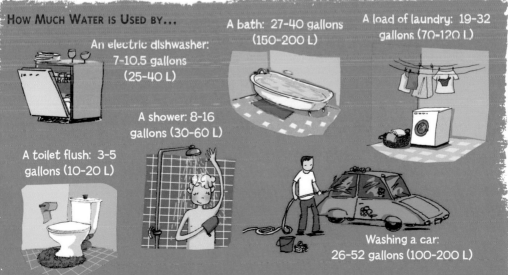

How Much Water is Used By...

An electric dishwasher: 7-10.5 gallons (25-40 L)

A bath: 27-40 gallons (150-200 L)

A load of laundry: 19-32 gallons (70-120 L)

A shower: 8-16 gallons (30-60 L)

A toilet flush: 3-5 gallons (10-20 L)

Washing a car: 26-52 gallons (100-200 L)

A Water Treatment Plant

Bathing, washing dishes and clothes and flushing toilets mean that water coming out of a house is dirty. Before sending it back into nature, this water must be cleaned to reduce the spread of germs or harmful substances. Water treatment plants also clean wastewater.

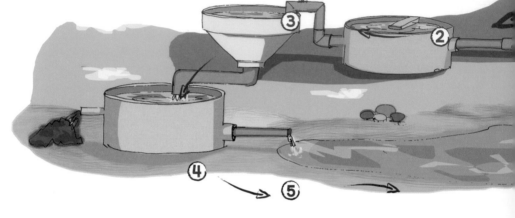

Make a Mini Water Treatment Plant

YOU WILL NEED:

- 2 pitchers
- Scissors
- Soil
- Coarse sand
- Gravel
- Blotting paper
- Some leaves and grass
- One clean flowerpot

1. Fill one pitcher with water and put in a little soil, sand, gravel, leaves and grass. Mix well.

① Wastewater drains from sewers into water mains. When it get to the water treatment plant*, it passes through a large grilled barrier which catches the largest pieces of waste material.

② The water flows into various tanks where it is cleansed of substances like sand, soil and (later) oily substances.

③ In another tank, the water is left to sit for several hours while particles known as "mud" sink to the bottom.

④ Next, the water must be cleaned with a biological treatment*, using microorganisms that feed on the remaining pollution.

⑤ In the final phase, the clean water is moved to another tank, leaving behind the sludge left by the biological treatment. The water can then be returned to the environment.

2. Put the flowerpot on the blotting paper and trace around the bottom. Cut out the circle you have drawn and put it in the bottom of the pot.

3. Fill the pot halfway up with the coarse sand and top it with a layer of gravel. Set the pot over the other (empty) pitcher.

4. Gently pour the dirty water mixture into the flowerpot. The sand and gravel will filter out some of the impurities. The water will come out cleaner, although not fit to drink.

In a water treatment plant, the water is purified as it passes through filters - each one finer than the last. Chemicals that kill germs are also added.

Our water resources are threatened by waste and pollution. As the number of inhabitants on Earth increases, so do the causes of water pollution.

Household Wastewater

Household activities — from bathing to laundry — produce dirty water, called "wastewater." Hospitals, schools and street-cleaning also create wastewater.

From the Field

Agriculture has become a growing source of pollution. The ground cannot absorb all of the nitrates from animal wastes produced in large "factory farms" and from the fertilizer* spread on crops. Pesticides* and herbicides* are other chemicals that the soil cannot absorb. All of these things can end up in rivers and groundwater.

Washed by Rain

Exhaust, motor oil and gasoline from roads can end up in the soil. These pollutants are dissolved in rainwater and contaminate ground water as they seep into the ground.

A Very Demanding Fish

Trout can only live in clean water with plenty of oxygen in it. If trout are found in a river or lake, it's proof that the water there is of high quality.

From Factories

Many factories that use water from rivers produce a great deal of wastewater — which may contain acids, metals and even radioactive particles. This can end up back in rivers even though much progress has been made in recent years to install anti-pollution equipment.

Make Acid Rain

YOU WILL NEED:
- 2 large jars
- 1 spray bottle
- 2 potted plants
- Labels
- Vinegar

2. Water the plants for several days — each with their own liquid. After a while, you will notice that the plant that gets pure water is healthy, while the one getting the water/vinegar mixture is doing badly.

1. Fill one jar with water and the other with a mixture of half water and half vinegar. Label one plant "Water" and label the other plant "Acid."

Water

Acid

Acid rains form when certain pollutants in the air — put there by cars or factories — mix into clouds. Acid rain has the effect on plants you observed in your experiment—it kills trees and also pollutes the rivers it falls into.

Water Contamination

If everything we throw into water, particularly bodily wastes, is not collected in sewers and treated, microorganisms will contaminate the water. These tiny germs can causes diseases in humans, and some are very serious.

WHAT IS AN ECOSYSTEM?

Life in a river or wetland is unbelievably well-organized. All sorts of plants and animals live together there, from large fish to tiny bugs. Each living thing has a role to play, and each finds nourishment there and contributes to the whole. There is a fragile balance in the system that pollution can completely destroy. The disappearance of one species can have serious consequences for all the others.

Water Can Kill

Certain algae love to feed on nitrates (which come from fertilizers) and phosphates (which come from detergents and other sources). When a large quantity of these products is present, too many of these algae grow, making the water green and choking out other forms of plants and animals. It is also suspected that absorbing too much of certain nitrates can cause cancer in humans.

The Food Chain

If a plant grows from polluted water, it will absorb the toxins contained in the water. A small fish that eats that plant will then absorb the pollutant. The small fish may be eaten by a bigger fish which will be caught and served to humans. This is how pollution moves up the food chain.

Protect Our Water

Here are some simple things you can do to help prevent water contamination.

* If you do projects around the house, avoid throwing away toxic products like paint. Put them aside to dispose of at your city's hazardous waste collection site.

* Other products like medicines and motor oil must also be disposed of at your city's hazardous waste collection site.
* In nature, never throw wastes in rivers or lakes.
* When shopping, choose biodegradable * cleaning products. And don't use more than you need!

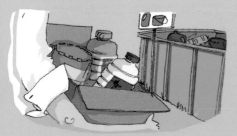

We must care for the planet's water because it is a treasure, essential for life. First, we must preserve our water sources like the underground aquifers, the rivers and springs, by polluting less - or not at all! Each of us can protect water in our daily lives. For example, you can avoid pouring toxic products down the drain.

Farming and Factories

It is possible to cultivate crops using fewer pesticides and fertilizers, and by choosing organic farming.

As for factories, they must come up with techniques to release fewer pollutants, and to treat their wastes before discharging them into waterways.

Make a Mini Oil Spill

YOU WILL NEED:
- A glass of cooking oil
- Ink
- A glass jar filled with water
- 1 old rag

colored oil

1. Pour the ink into the oil to color it. Then pour the glass of oil in the jar. What do you observe?

Stop Leaks!
A dripping faucet can waste up to 8 gallons (300 L) of water a day!

Oil Spills
The Exxon Valdez oil spill in 1989 killed an estimated 300,000 birds.

Reducing Waste

Certain factories try to lessen their water consumption by using a "closed circuit" system. Water polluted by chemical products is treated and reused. At home, you can reduce water waste by taking quick showers (this uses less water than baths) and by getting rid of all water leaks.

WATER LAWS
The Clean Water Act of 1972 set down the guidelines that govern how water is treated in the United States. Other water laws vary by state and town. For example, during a drought, a town may decide that people may only water their lawns once a week in order to save water.

2. Oil floats on water. That's because water is more dense* than oil.

3. If you stick an old rag into the jar, you will see that, little by little, the rag absorbs the colored oil.

colored oil
water

After an oil spill, oil spreads over the surface of the water in thick layers which sticks to birds' feathers. But oil also contains products that are denser than water, which drop to the bottom of the ocean, which means that fish are also affected by oil spills.

Water for the Future

The world's population is growing. In just 100 years, it will have multiplied 3 times and worldwide water usage will be 7 times greater! But the Earth's reserves of freshwater can't increase. Do the math. Each person's amount of available water will be reduced. But that's not all...

Lack of Water

The greater a population's quality of life, the greater its water usage, because more people have things like clothes washers and dishwashers. Plus, today's farming techniques are increasing our use of water, particularly in developed countries like the United States and in Europe. The number of highways is also increasing, and bringing more pollution with them. Throughout the world, the populations of cities grow and their wastewater is not always properly treated before ending up in rivers.

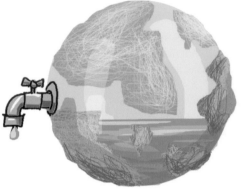

WATER USE AROUND THE WORLD
(DAILY USE, PER PERSON)

Africa: 8 gallons (30 L)

North America:
152 gallons (575 L)

Europe: 66 gallons
(250 L)

Water in the World

Water is not distributed equally across the Earth. It rains too much in certain areas, which causes catastrophic floods. In desert regions, it almost never rains. In these areas, people must travel dozens of miles (km) in search of water. Women and children sometimes walk several hours each day to reach the nearest well to bring back water to their families. They must do this because digging a well is very expensive.

Construct a Well or Spring

YOU WILL NEED:
- 1 small saucer
- 1 sponge
- 2 paper towels
- 1 sheet of plastic wrap
- Soil
- 1 thin, sturdy straw or tube

2. Lay the plastic wrap on top and then the soil. Pierce through all the layers with the straw. You have "dug" a well.

1. On the saucer, layer the sponge and paper towels. Pour on 2 or 3 glasses of water.

3. The sponge, the cloth, the plastic wrap and the plate represent the different layers beneath the Earth's surface. When you tip the plate to one side, the water flows out. That's how a spring works.

Warring over Water

Water is essential for everyone and it is a resource that belongs to everyone. Water has no boundaries. Many rivers or other bodies of water are shared by several countries. But because the scarcity of freshwater is a real problem in several regions in the world, water has caused serious conflicts between different groups.

Blue Gold

Studies show that, in years to come, water will become like "blue gold" that people will fight over. Some countries in Asia and Africa have already gone to war over access to rivers or over the control mountains or plains rich in water resources. Such wars have become more common in the last 50 years.

Make a River Collage

You will need:
- A drawing pad
- Colored pencils
- Glue
- Cardboard

Visit a river bank and collect samples of what you find there (pebbles, bird feathers, fallen leaves). Then make a picture by drawing in your river and gluing on objects you have found in nature.

Water Stress

This is the expression specialists use to describe the current situation of the water supply on Earth.

What Nationality?

River water is often shared by several countries. For example, the waters of the Rhine River are shared by France, Germany, Switzerland and the Netherlands, and the waters of the Niagara River are shared by the United States and Canada.

Different Techniques

Researchers are trying to develop new methods to find water in places where it is scarce. For example, they are trying to take the salt out of sea water. This method (which is very expensive) already exists in several countries such as Kuwait, Saudi Arabia and Israel. In Chile, they "capture" fog with huge nets stretched across mountainsides. Elsewhere, people are installing ingenious rooftop systems to capture rainwater.

The Death of the Aral Sea

The Aral Sea was in a region of Uzbekistan. Then, 30 years ago, dams were built on the two rivers that fed into the sea. In just a few years, the water level dropped by half and the water became extremely salty. Little by little, this sea is dying and the area around it is becoming a desert that no longer supports life.

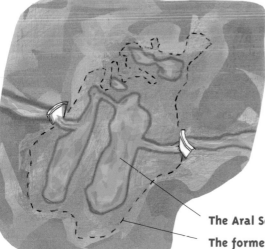

The Aral Sea today

The former size of the Aral Sea

Maybe you would like to work in a field in which you could help protect water. There are people, such as fishermen or sailors, who work on the water. There are also people who work on behalf of water. Below are 2 examples:

FARMING IN WATER

Someone who works in aquaculture, or fish farming, raises fish to sell. Schools of trout, carp and pike live in special tanks. Their feeding and breeding are managed – a little like the raising of sheep or cows. But it's very important that aquatic farmers don't release their wastewater into neighboring rivers.

Water Expert

A hydrobiologist is both an engineer and a specialist in water ecology. Such people study the state of a body of water, its pollution level and the consequences of that pollution on the fish and plants – all the living organisms in the river's water. The hydrobiologist proposes solutions to increase living things in the water or to clean the water in a way that is good for the environment.

Observe the River

There are several signs that show when a river is polluted. Here are some that you can easily observe:

- The water is murky or it has an odor other than the normal scent of a riverbed.
- There are no fish (worse yet, there are dead fish).
- A lack of insects and the presence of worms in the riverbed.
- The presence of any sort of garbage
- Large quantities of green algae

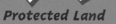

Protected Land

In 1959, Antarctica obtained a unique status as an International Zone. By treaty, this area has become a natural reserve dedicated to peace and science.

The Return of the Beaver

The European beaver was hunted for its fur and nearly became extinct. However, over the last several years beavers have been reintroduced in the wild in several parts of Europe.

Guardians of Water

There are people whose job it is to take care of rivers and keep them clean. These "river guards" clear brush from river banks, tend the paths and restore springs. In the same way, "coastal guards" work to protect the health of seashores.

Glossary

biodegradable: Something that can be broken down, or eaten by tiny living organisms, in a natural process.

biological treatment: This is a process that uses living things to clean water. Tiny organisms eat the dirt and pollutants, cleaning the water naturally.

dense: A measure of something's relative mass (weight) compared to its volume.

fertilizer: Substances that enriches the soil to help cultivated plants thrive.

groundwater: When rain falls, some of the water seeps into the soil until it reaches a layer of impenetrable rock. Groundwater collected in underground reserves (aquifers) is an important source of water around the world.

herbicide: Chemical products that kill weeds and other unwanted plants.

medicinal properties: Qualities which treat certain diseases.

minerals: Food and drinking water provide us with minerals, which are necessary for life. Among these minerals are sodium, potassium, calcium, and iron.

nutrients: Chemical elements essential for growth in living organisms.

oil spill: The accidental or intentional release of petroleum products into the environment. They are caused by human activities like oil drilling, production, storage and transport.

organic farming: Agricultural practices that respect the environment.

pesticide: Chemical product which kills insects and certain plants.

water treatment plant: An installation designed to treat wastewater before returning it to rivers or the ocean. However, this treated water may not be safe to drink.

To Learn More:

Books:

Bowden, Rob. *Earth's Water Crisis*. Milwaukee, WI:
World Almanac Library, 2007.

Kerley, Barbara. *A Cool Drink of Water*. Des Moines, IA: National Geographic
Children's Books, 2006.

Strauss, Rochelle. *One Well: The Story of Water on Earth*. Toronto: Kids Can Press,
2007.

On the Internet:

To ensure the currency and safety of
recommended Internet links, Windmill
maintains and updates an online list of
sites related to the subject of this book.
To access this list of Web sites, please go
to www.windmillbooks.com/weblinks and
select this book's title.

For more great fiction
and nonfiction, go to
windmillbooks.com